Natural I

Anna Haycraft live with her publisher h family which she br just such recipes as she describes in this book. With Caroline Blackwood she is the author of another cookery book, *Darling, You Shouldn't Have Gone to So Much Trouble*. She has also written four novels, under the pseudonym Alice Thomas Ellis.

Natural
Baby Food

ANNA HAYCRAFT

FONTANA/COLLINS

First published by Gerald Duckworth & Co. Ltd 1977
First issued in Fontana Paperbacks 1980
Third impression August 1983
Fourth impression, in this format, April 1985

Copyright © Anna Haycraft 1977
Set in Linotype Pilgrim

Made and printed in Great Britain by
William Collins Sons & Co. Ltd, Glasgow

Contents

Conversion Table

Electricity		Gas
150°C/300°F	=	2
160°C/325°F	=	3
180°C/350°F	=	4
190°C/375°F	=	5
200°C/400°F	=	6
220°C/425°F	=	7
230°C/450°F	=	8

Introduction

Breast-feeding

Most mothers do not breast-feed their babies. A recent spot check in one maternity ward revealed that six out of the eight women were not even prepared to consider it. Reasons varied from the fear of being made to 'feel like a cow' to doubt that it would ever be possible to know when the baby had had enough. One mother admitted that she thought there was something 'mucky' in such intimate contact with an infant, and one thought it 'old-fashioned'. When questioned further she said that she also thought it 'common'.

In modern society the breast has ceased to be a maternal symbol and has become a sexual symbol. Thus topless waitresses and bare-breasted models are acceptable, while breast-feeding, especially in public, is a matter for embarrassment. Then again for financial reasons many mothers need to return to work soon after the birth of their babies. This problem is recognized and discussed in a report on infant feeding issued in the UK by the Department of Health.*

* *Present-day Practice in Infant-feeding*, Report on Health and Social Subjects No. 9, London HMSO 1974.

which strongly urges measures to promote breast-feeding.

Another factor which influences mothers is that breast-fed babies usually stay slim, and slimness in babies is unfashionable. There is a tendency to think that only a fat baby can be healthy. Afraid that their own milk supply may be inadequate, many mothers take readily to bottle-feeding and are soon supplementing it with fattening cereals and tinned foods. The baby who takes to these is regarded as a compliant, good baby. But overweight in infants is only too common, and the result can be a lifelong weight problem.

Although there seems to be a revival of interest in breast-feeding, a mother may still find it difficult to get information on the subject unless she happens to have a sympathetic GP. She may well receive contradictory advice from official sources as well as misleading ideas from friends and relations. Yet there are actually very few cases where physical factors prevent breast-feeding. Mother's milk is not just another secretion, an inconvenient side-effect of childbirth. It is the natural, and best possible, nourishment for your baby – and the cheapest and most convenient method of feeding.

Despite the advances made in artificial milk feeds, especially the 'ready-to-feed' variety used mostly by hospitals, the claim that these products are 'as good as' or even 'superior to' breast milk is simply untrue. No manufactured product reproduces all the advantages of human milk for the new-born baby. The mother who breast-feeds her baby for even a short time is contributing a great deal to her child's development and future health.

Apart from the psychological and emotional aspects, which are outside the scope of this book, perhaps the most important argument for breast-feeding is associated with questions of infection and immunity. Bottle-feeding obviously introduces a great risk of contamination and of error in the preparation of feeds. But studies have shown that breast-fed babies also have fewer illnesses than bottle-fed babies. For instance the link between breast-feeding and resistance to gastro-enteritis is now well-established : statistics show that only a very small proportion of deaths from enteritis in the first year occur in babies who have been breast-fed. Many authorities hold that breast milk contains antibodies that help to protect the infant from infection at a particularly vulnerable stage of life – for example, against the poliomyelitis virus.

Breast-feeding also ensures that the baby is not exposed, at a vulnerable age, to the allergens which may be present in cow's milk. The younger the baby, the more likely there is to be some deficiency in the immunological defence mechanism, and it has been suggested that some chronic allergies may derive from exposure to allergens in cow's milk and other foods before immunity has built up.

Most artificial milk feeds are based on cow's milk,

traditionally the most acceptable substitute for human milk. But its composition is quite different from that of human milk. A calf grows and develops to maturity in a little over two years, and the composition of cow's milk is geared to maintain this rapid growth. The human child, on the other hand, develops very slowly, and correspondingly human milk is designed for slow growth. Even in modified form, cow's milk makes excessive demands on the physiological adaptability of the infant, especially in the first few weeks of life.

Cow's milk contains roughly the same level of fat as human milk, but nearly twice as much protein. It is higher in phosphate and calcium, and it has a greater concentration of sodium and potassium – elements likely to place an increased strain on the baby's kidneys. The composition of the fat content also differs from that of human milk, and butterfat is not well absorbed by the human infant. Breast milk is richer in polyunsaturated acids, and this could be of importance to the growth of the developing brain.

The tough casein curd of cow's milk is larger and less digestible for the human body and has been known to cause intestinal blockage in babies. The young baby's digestive tract has to work harder to use the protein of cow's milk, the excess being passed on through the intestines to form the odorous large-curd stool characteristic of bottle-fed babies. The inoffensive-smelling stool of the breast-fed baby is acidic, and discourages the growth of bacteria which cause nappy rash, whereas cow's milk tends to produce an alkaline stool in which these bacteria multiply.

So breast-feed your baby if you possibly can. A number of organizations interested in promoting the practice of breast-feeding now exist and if you want further information or advice, write to the National Childbirth Trust, 9 Queensborough Terrace, London W2. The Trust's Breast-Feeding Promotion Group has members throughout the country, and the London office will give you the name of your nearest representative. The La Leche League, an American organization promoting breast-feeding, also has a branch in the UK.

Mixed feeding

The introduction of solid food before the age of six months may well be a danger to health, and should be avoided. While it is true that the digestive system of a very young baby can tolerate a wide range of foods, there is no medical evidence that the development or health of the baby is benefited by early weaning. On the contrary, evidence suggests that it can sometimes be positively harmful, and not only from the danger of obesity. Recent investigations have pointed to a connection between early introduction of solids and the incidence of coeliac disease in children. A recent survey of a group of children in Scotland suffering from the disease showed that a high percentage of them had been fed wheat cereals in the first months, some before one month.

Mothers who bottle-feed their babies seem particularly prone to over-feed them in the early months, adding cereals to their diet far too soon, sometimes when the child is only a few weeks old.

When the time does come to go on to mixed feeding – preferably when the baby is about six months old, but certainly not before four months – it is very tempting to rely exclusively on commercial baby foods. But although these products can be useful when there is really no time to cook, there is no reason why in normal times your baby should not eat virtually the same foods as the rest of the family, with a few differences in preparation. This not only saves money, but lays the foundation for proper food habits from the start, as well as avoiding the problem of the additives, chemicals and distorted flavours in manufactured baby foods.

It is never too early to start forming proper food habits. As children grow older the problem of getting them to eat the right food becomes more difficult. On television they will see advertised an astonishing variety of chocolates, sweets, artificial gravies, tinned meats, bottled sauces, starchy puddings, sliced bread, biscuits and sugary drinks. They will pass sweet shops on every shopping trip and the supermarket will display all the things they have seen. These will be that much harder to resist if the child's taste has already become accustomed to processed foods which, when not hopelessly bland, are over-seasoned or over-sweetened. Food habits are among the hardest to change, and this is one of the best reasons for doing your own cooking for your baby from the beginning.

Commercial baby 'dinners' often have as their main ingredient cereal, unenriched rice or other starchy substances. These fill and fatten, but do not particularly nourish the child. Baby foods are flavoured to appeal to the mother, and unnecessary amounts of salt or sugar are added. Sufficient salt for babies is present naturally in milk, many vegetables, meat, fish and cheese; yet processed baby foods sometimes contain at least five times as much salt as there is in fresh meat, and from twelve to twenty times as much salt as in breast milk.

There is evidence that the early consumption of salt can lead to increased desire for salt in later life and to hypertension in adulthood. Moreover, salt has recently been suggested as a cause of cot deaths – where the baby is found dead for no apparent reason. A survey of 54 cot deaths* established that 52 of the children were dehydrated, possibly as a result of the high salt content in many baby foods. It is uncertain whether dehydration was the sole cause of death or whether it simply made the child less resistant to a

* *Journal of Medicine, Science and Law*, February 1975.

minor infection; but mothers should be aware of the presence of salt in baby foods and in other processed foods, and give babies plenty to drink.

Some baby foods are grossly oversweetened, as are many commercial foods – not merely puddings and fruit drinks but also so-called savoury foods such as tinned spaghetti and beans, bottled mayonnaise, and soups. Cyclamates have now been banned, but *all* sweetening agents can lead to addiction. Refined white sugar can be seen as a real threat to health. It undoubtedly causes both tooth decay and obesity, and although no casual relationship has been proved, its vastly increased consumption is correlated with the increase in coronary heart disease and arterio-sclerosis. It can also cause an over-production of insulin, which creates a craving for more sugar – a vicious circle that can lead to diabetes in susceptible people. Both brown and white sugar are refined – white more than brown. Black treacle is a by-product of sugar manufacture, and contains sucrose, but it also retains a number of nutrients and is preferable as a sweetener. Honey is a natural sweetener, sweeter than sugar, and it contains some trace elements and vitamins. While it is probably as deleterious to the teeth as refined sugar if taken in the same quantities, the fact that it has a taste, apart from its mere sweet-ness, means that you can use much less of it to make a dish appetizing – as it can enhance, rather than smother, flavour. Therefore baby food should be sweetened very sparingly, and whenever possible with honey; or when appropriate, dried fruits may be used.

Besides sugar and salt, there are many other dubious additives in use, such as modified starch, which some babies have difficulty in digesting, and the stabilizers put in to prevent baby foods from separating into their constituent parts. Monosodium glutamate has recently been banned from baby foods, but it is still present in other processed foods which mothers might use to supplement their baby's diet. This is particularly true of stock cubes, which should be avoided for this reason.

In Canada and France, excess nitrates were discovered in prepared baby vegetables. These are particularly dangerous to babies under three months old, as they change to nitrites in the immature digestive system and are then absorbed into the blood. There they set off a process which interferes with the red blood cells' ability to carry oxygen; in high amounts, they could cause suffocation.

Canning and processing can also destroy vitamins. Vitamin C is the chief victim, but other heat-sensitive vitamins may be lost. Vitamin C is replaced by the manufacturer, but it may be destroyed again when an anti-oxidant is introduced to prolong the shelf-life of the product. (Tinned foods, even now, are not date-stamped for the consumer and may well be much older than the baby eating them; potentially dangerous preservatives are added to ensure this long life.) If the product claims to have 'extra Vitamin C', it may be found to contain a ludicrously large amount. Water-soluble vitamins are discarded when the liquid from tinned vegetables is poured off, while baby foods packed in clear glass jars are liable to be deficient in Vitamins B2 and B6 which are sensitive to light.

Even liquid paraffin, which has been used for many years to give packaged raisins and sultanas a gloss and stop them sticking together, has been found to have harmful long-term effects, attacking the lining of the stomach and preventing the absorption of useful vitamins – although it once had a respectable place in the household as a standard opening medicine. Producers are at present experimenting with substitutes, but meanwhile packaged dried fruits should be carefully washed before use.

The Ministry of Agriculture, Fisheries and Food keeps a check on the cumulative effects of chemicals used in manufactured foods and issues lists of permitted additives. But it admits that it can only advise with reservations on the safety of substances, since safety is impossible to prove in any absolute sense.

Unfortunately, even if you make everything at home and avoid processed foods, there are still some dangers inherent in 'natural' foods, and the raw materials of cooking must be chosen carefully. Fresh meat and vegetables may contain hormones or poisonous weed-killers, and there is no way of avoiding the ever-present insecticides. If possible, it is a good idea to buy unsprayed or organically grown vegetables, and always to wash vegetables and fruit well in warm water and then rinse in running water.

Use wholemeal flour whenever possible, and buy or bake wholemeal bread. White flour is devoid of most of the trace minerals and many of the vitamins contained in whole-grain flours. These flours, together with fibrous vegetables, provide vital roughage – another deficiency in packaged diets. Try to use sea or kosher salt, which taste better than ordinary table salt and are not bleached or treated with chemicals to make them pour without caking.

The relative values of various types of oils and fats available are not fully understood. Fears about the effects of cholesterol have led many people to advocate the elimination of saturated fats from male diets, but it should be remembered that cholesterol is used by the body in the manufacture of sex hormones, vitamin D from sunlight, and bile acids. It only becomes a hazard when excessive amounts are built up and secreted in the blood vessels, and various studies have shown that the greatest single cause of this is lack of exercise. It is probably wisest to buy saturated and unsaturated fats and use both in moderation. In general fats having a low melting point – i.e. those which are liquid at room temperature – are less saturated than those which are solid at room temperature.

Finding *pure* fats and oils is a problem. Pure butter has no additives, but margarine has emulsifiers, preservatives, colouring and flavouring added, and some brands have as high a saturated fat content as butter. Of the vegetable oils, olive oil is usually without additives, but many other types contain preservative.

By using common sense and discrimination it is still possible to get value for your money. On the whole fresh unprocessed foods cost less than processed prepared foods and are better, safer and tastier.

When the baby is ready for solid food, buy some small, shallow spoons and a fork, some unbreakable baby dishes and some large bibs. Make sure all utensils are rinsed well free of detergents.

An invaluable aid to the making of cheaper and better home-made juices, soups, purées etc., is a liquidizer/blender. The initial cost will soon be justified by the savings on the grocery bill, and while it is not essential to the preparation of baby food – a sieve or mill are good substitutes – it is quicker and easier. If you have a home freezer, several of the recipes in this book are suitable for freezing.

Note on the recipes

I have nowhere attempted to lay down a rigid schedule for the introduction of mixed feeding. Chapter 1, on first solid foods, starts from the premise that a healthy breast-fed baby will not need any food other than mother's milk for the first six months of life, and gives advice about vitamin and iron supplements. My aim is to offer general guidelines for a successful transition to solids which will bring your baby to the stage where he is eating more or less what the whole family eats. Since the introduction of solids before six months is not recommended here, particular references to the 'young baby' in the recipes should be taken to apply to children between six and nine months old.

The remaining recipes in the book have been grouped according to the main ingredient (meat, fish etc.) roughly in the order in which these are likely to be introduced into the baby's diet. They fall into two categories: those which provide a small individual meal for the baby; and those for the family as a whole, which, with slight adjustments, can be offered to the baby as well.

When preparing a casserole, stew or pudding to be cooked in the oven, it is often easier to make a tiny individual one specially for the baby, since this allows you to leave out any ingredients not yet introduced into his diet. You can buy small, lidded casserole dishes, or cover ramekins with transparent roasting wrap. These very small quantities cook in half the time or less, so put them in after the main dish. Or, with a young baby, you can often use some of the stock thickened with a little potato, to extend his range of familiar flavours; later, you can select those ingredients of the main meal which you have already introduced into the baby's diet, and blend or sieve them with the stock or a little home-made gravy. Do not use commercial gravy powders.

When cooking for the whole family it is better to add salt after the baby's portion has been taken out of the main dish. As a reminder, amounts of salt are bracketed in the following recipes.

When you begin a new food, include it in the baby's diet at least once a week to encourage familiarity, unless the baby shows an adverse reaction. If you wait four or five days after the introduction of each new food, you will know the cause of any symptoms of an allergy.

IMPORTANT: *Note on Milk and Grain*

A number of nutritionists are re-considering the role of milk as a normal item of diet. (It is, after all, designed by nature as a food for the infants of a particular species.) They have discovered that 50% of white babies, 70% of black babies and 100% Chinese lose the enzyme and therefore the capacity for digesting milk round about the age of 12 months. Therefore should a baby show signs of allergy after this time, always remember to consider milk as a possible cause.

It is in any case advisable not to think of milk as a drink but to offer a thirsty child water or a *moderate* amount of diluted fruit juice.

Grain and grain products are another frequently unsuspected but common cause of allergy.

1. First Solid Foods

For some years there has been an unfortunate trend towards earlier and earlier introduction of solids. Mothers compete to see who can start their babies on solids first, and the mother is admired who manages to stuff the greatest variety of prepared baby food into her baby at the youngest age.

This is not only unnecessary, it is unwise. An infant's digestive tract is not ready for solid food until it is at least three months old, and a breast-fed baby does not need solids for up to six months or more. A normal full-term baby born to a mother whose diet and health are good should have enough iron stored in the liver to last for about six months. Only after this is there any need for iron in the form of meat, cereals and egg yolks. Even the bottle-fed baby may need nothing but milk for the first three to four months, though both breast- and bottle-fed babies probably need supplementary vitamins. It is usually best to nurse or bottle-feed the baby before each meal of solids until at least seven or eight months. Milk is still most important to babies at this time and should be given while they are still hungry.

Vitamins

The quantity of vitamin D present in human and cow's milk is too small to form an adequate protection against rickets, and while this is not a problem in climates where the child can be out of doors with the sunshine falling directly on the skin, it is a problem in colder countries, especially in winter, and in towns. Bottle-fed babies will not need supplements of the fat-soluble vitamins A and D, because these are added to their milk powders. Breast-fed babies in this country should be given vitamin drops, especially in the winter months. The water-soluble vitamin C is present in breast milk and is added to milk powders. It is therefore not necessary while the baby is on these milks.

The vitamin drops available at present contain A, C and D. Bottle-fed babies do not need the supplement, because dried milk is fortified. They can, however, have a half-dosage without harm – excess vitamin C is simply excreted in the urine, and while excess vitamin D can be harmful, the dosage would have to be very great and for a long period.

It is important to realize that the vitamin drops provide all the extra vitamins your child needs. There is therefore no need to buy expensive fruit concentrates. In fact these contain *only* vitamin C, which would simply be excreted. These very sweet juices can also harm the developing teeth. In all too many cases the baby graduates from these to soft drinks (containing additives) and never develops the habit of drinking water. Remember also that babies often cry from thirst rather than hunger. This can be due to milk feeds being over-concentrated, or later to food being too salty. Boiled water should be given, since, once again, commercial fruit concentrates are expensive, and unnecessary.

Fruit

Banana, mashed with a fork or put through the blender, is a useful way of introducing the first new texture and flavour to the baby's diet. Apple purée can soon be introduced as a variation on banana, simply by scraping the pulp from a peeled apple, or by making an unsweetened apple sauce. A new fruit can be introduced every four days or so. Peaches, apricots and pears are a good choice among the commonly available fruits, and of course fresh, unsweetened juice may be started at the same time as the fruit (or vegetable) from which it comes.

Egg yolk

This is a useful food to introduce early to replenish diminishing supplies of iron (see above, p. 21). The egg is probably best hard-boiled, as it is slightly easier to digest than when soft-boiled. Remove the yolk and sieve it. It can be mixed with a little boiled milk to give it a creamy texture. Only a teaspoon or two should be offered at first.

Meat

Buy iron-rich meat such as liver, and make sure it is lean and well-cooked. Sieve or blend the meat with a little stock or gravy, and give only a teaspoon or two at first. You can introduce a new meat every five to seven days, alternating with those already tried.

Fish

Be careful to remove all skin and bone from the fish, and make sure that it is well-cooked. (For suitable

varieties of fish and cooking methods, see p. 56.)
Purée it with a little stock, and again give only a teaspoon or two at first. Fish can of course be mashed
with potato or other vegetables once these have been
introduced into the baby's diet.

Vegetables

You can begin quite early mashing a little potato with
some of the stock or gravy from the family meal, but
certain vegetables should be avoided in the early
stages because they can cause flatulence. (For suitable
first vegetables see p. 63.) Add these, one at a time,
to the baby's main meal, mashed or blended with
their cooking liquid.

Tomato juice or purée can be introduced at about
eight months. Tomatoes are a rich source of vitamin
C and an appetizing base to soups and stews.

Cereals

As mentioned earlier, because of the danger of obesity
and other attendant risks, it is usually best to delay
giving cereals until your baby is eight or nine months

old, and choose instead other high iron and protein foods. If, however, the child has a tendency to diarrhoea or is gaining weight so slowly that your doctor feels a filling food is essential, you may wish to begin cereals earlier. Even then, if the baby is under six months, it is better to avoid the high-gluten content wheat-based cereals, and also pre-cooked cereals, since they can cause digestive difficulties and stomach pains in the very young baby. Keep to natural-grain cereals if you possibly can; otherwise look for the whole-grain and unsweetened brands.

Teething

As the baby develops the urge to chew, you can start to make food coarser. Do not buy over-sweetened commercial teething biscuits. Crusts, toasts or rusks (fingers of bread hardened in a slow oven) are best, and if these are made from home-made bread or rolls, so much the better (For a recipe for teething biscuits see page 102.)

You can begin to offer small sips of cow's milk from a cup with each meal when the baby is seven or eight months old. But don't be tempted to force more than the baby seems to want, and as the months go by be careful not to overrate the nutritional value of milk. Milk alone will not function as a complete diet, and the need for other, especially iron-rich, foods will increase.

By the time the baby is nine months old you will be able to see the outlines of the three balanced meals an older child would have. For example, a simple menu for a child of eight to twelve months might be:

Breakfast
orange juice
egg yolk (or whole egg)
cooked cereals (as needed)
milk

Lunch
meat or fish
vegetables
fruit, pudding, yoghourt or custard
milk

Tea
grated cheese or soup
fruit
whole-grain bread
milk

2. *Fruit*

Suitable fruits and methods of preparation

Some nutrients are destroyed when fruit is cooked so it is sensible to eat as much as possible raw. Babies can drink the juice – diluted with a little boiled water if the fruit is very acid. Since the skin is high in vitamin content, peel thinly. Cooked fruit retains more nutrients if unpeeled. Cook gently for as short a time as possible and sweeten as little as possible (you can stew fruit in a syrup of honey and water), and then strain through a sieve or food mill. All fruit should first be well washed in warm water.

Bananas – bland, smooth and digestible (choose the ripe, brown, speckled sort) – and apple purée have already been mentioned as a suitable introduction to a mixed diet. Oranges, apricots, peaches, pears, grapefruit, pineapple, melon, black or red currants (cooked and strained), prunes and dried apricots may all be gradually added to the menu. For older babies, strawberries, raspberries and blackberries (with the pips strained out), raisins, sultanas and dates are suitable. Dried fruits, particularly apricots, are rich in iron. (Wash well before use.)

Suitable juices

Orange, apple, apricot, grapefruit, tomato, black-currant, pineapple, and most vegetables.

Stewed apples

Use apples that go soft and pulpy when cooked; wash them well in warm water, quarter them, cut out the blemishes and stew them in their skins, using very little water. Cook gently until quite soft; then sieve or mill. Cook without sugar, sweetening with a little honey. Pears can also be cooked in this way.

Baked apples

Wash apples well, remove cores and replace with sultanas or raisins. Cook at 360° for about half an hour to an hour, depending on size, or until soft. Sieve the baby's portion.

Dried fruit

Dried fruit, such as prunes and apricots, must be well washed in warm water to remove any particles of grit and traces of liquid paraffin or preservative. You can cook them very slowly in the bottom of the oven in a lidded casserole dish in sufficient water to cover them. If you leave them to soak overnight, use the same water to cook them in. You may need to add a little brown sugar – about 3 oz to the lb – or honey.

3. Meat

There is absolutely no need to buy expensive meat. In the following recipes I have placed the emphasis on the cheaper cuts, which tend to be more nourishing and, properly prepared, equally delicious. Rabbit in particular is both nutritious and very good value for money.

If you are anxious about antibiotics, artificial hormones and chemical additives, you may be able to find a butcher who guarantees naturally raised meat. Needless to say, canned and processed meat has further chemicals, preservatives and colourants added.

Suitable meat for babies

Braise, stew, or casserole : rabbit, beef, chicken, lamb, heart, kidney, liver, tongue, sweetbreads, tripe, brains.
Roast : beef, chicken, lamb, turkey.
Grill : chicken, kidney, liver, lamb chops, steak.

Do not give prepared meat, such as sausages, salami, corned beef, frankfurters, luncheon meat or other canned meat. Do not give pork, ham or bacon until the baby is older.

To prepare meat for babies under nine months old

1. Be sure the meat is well cooked, but not over-cooked.
2. Remove any fat or gristle, skin or bone.
3. Put enough water or stock in the blender to cover the blades.
4. Dice the meat and add it to the liquid.
5. Blend until the mixture is of the desired consistency – puréed for younger, and coarser for older babies. Soft meat can be sieved. Do not add salt until you have removed the baby's portion. Never give babies meat that has been re-heated more than once. Food to be re-heated should be cooled quickly after the first cooking, covered, and re-frigerated as soon as possible. If you do re-heat, make sure that you do it thoroughly, that is, bring to the boil and then simmer for at least 20 minutes. Bacteria flourish in inadequately cooked meat dishes.

Once meat is a regular part of the child's diet, you can cut off a little of the family roast or stew and blend or sieve it with some of the gravy – don't worry if the gravy has been made with onion; this won't upset a baby who has not been started on mixed feeding too early.

BEEF TEA (*Mrs Beeton's recipe*)

Mrs Beeton's beef tea can be a useful and nourishing standby when you are introducing meat into the baby's diet. The following recipe makes one pint. Any surplus makes an excellent stock for a casserole or can be served as soup. The meat can be eaten with potatoes or other vegetables, or used as a filling for pasties (see p. 49).

> 1 lb fleshy beef
> 1 pint water

Trim off the fat and cut the beef into small cubes. Place it with water in a baking-dish or jar with a tight-fitting lid in a warm, but not hot, oven and bake for 3 to 4 hours. Strain and put in a cool place [refrigerator]. (The tea can be flavoured with an onion, a clove or herbs.)

Liver

Try to serve liver at least once a week. It is an invaluable source of iron. All types are equally nutritious and there is no need to buy the most expensive. Liver, like minced beef, should be cooked either for a very short time, or for a very long time; otherwise it will be hard. Grill a small slice (about 2oz) for a few minutes on each side. Blend or sieve.

LIVER AND POTATO SHAPE

1 lb liver
small onion
1 lb potatoes

(½ teaspoon salt)
pinch mixed herbs

Grill the liver, remove any connective tissue and put it through the fine blade of a mincer or blender. Having steamed or boiled the potatoes with the onion, mash them and mix with the liver, if necessary moistening with stock or milk. Heat it through in a small loaf tin, either in the oven at 350°, or standing in a covered pan half full of water on top of the stove.

For the young baby, mash a little with a teaspoon of stock or boiled milk. You can make a complete dinner by adding cooked and mashed vegetables, chosen according to age.

LIVER STEW

1 lb liver	1 tablespoon
4 large tomatoes	chopped parsley
(½ teaspoon salt)	1 small onion
½ lb carrots	

Slice the liver, peel the tomatoes, peel and slice the carrots and onion and either cook in a covered casserole dish in the oven at 350° for 50 minutes, or simmer in a covered pan on top of the stove over a low heat for 30 or 40 minutes or until tender. Remove the baby's portion and blend, sieve or chop it.

BEEF AND LIVER LOAF

¾ lb liver
1 ½ lb minced beef
2 tablespoons rolled
   oats
1 medium-sized
   onion

½ pint pure
   tomato juice
1 egg or egg yolk
(½ teaspoon salt)

Mince or blend the liver and onion, mix thoroughly with the mince, rolled oats, tomato juice and egg. Form into a loaf in a greased, medium-sized loaf tin. Bake at 350° for 1 hour. Blend or chop the baby's portion with a little liquid. This dish can also be served cold to older babies.

FAGGOTS

Roll the above mixture into egg-sized balls. Put into a casserole dish and pour over ½ pint of meat or vegetable stock. Cover and cook at 350° for 1 hour. Blend or chop the baby's portion.

Kidneys

Kidneys are nutritious, easily digestible, and not too expensive. To prepare them, remove the outer membrane, split and remove the tubules.

Lamb kidney

Put enough water in a small saucepan to cover the bottom and add the chopped kidney, prepared as above. Bring it to the boil, lower the heat, cover and simmer for about 10 minutes, or until tender. Blend or sieve with the cooking juices, or chop finely and serve with mashed potato or any other vegetable suitable for the baby's age and diet. The kidneys can also be lightly grilled, about 5 minutes on each side.

STEAK AND KIDNEY STEW

1 lb stewing steak	½ lb onions
½ lb kidney	½ pint water or
1 tablespoon oil	stock
1 tablespoon	(½ teaspoon salt)
wholemeal flour	

Cut up the meat, removing any gristle or fat, roll it in wholemeal flour and fry lightly in the oil. Put it into a casserole dish with the chopped onions, add the liquid and cover tightly with foil and lid. Cook in the oven at about 350° for 2 hours, or until tender. Remove the baby's portion and blend or chop it, according to age. Season the remainder.

STEAK AND KIDNEY PUDDING

crust

½ lb wholemeal
   flour
1 teaspoon baking
   powder

½ teaspoon salt
3 oz suet

filling

1 lb stewing steak
1 tablespoon
   wholemeal flour
1 small chopped
   onion

2 sheep's kidneys
(1 ½ teaspoons
   salt)
2-3 tablespoons
   stock or water

Make the crust by mixing the ingredients then adding cold water to form a soft, but not sticky, dough.

Grease a pudding basin and line it with the dough. Cut up the meat and dip each piece in flour. Put it in the basin and add stock or water. Damp the edges of the crust and make a top with the remaining dough. Steam for 3 hours, or longer if the meat is tough. Blend or chop, omitting the pastry, for the younger baby. This is a very nutritious way of cooking meat.

Heart

Heart is nutritious, low-priced and full of flavour. It can be stewed, roasted or casseroled, but needs long, slow cooking. Ox heart, which is enough for 5 to 6 servings, takes 2 to 3 hours; sheep or lamb heart. which will serve 1 to 2 people, takes 1½ to 2 hours. Wash the heart well in several changes of cold water, remove the membranous flaps and tubes, and wash clear of all blood. Soak in water for at least half an hour.

STEWED HEART

4 sheep's hearts
½ pint stock or
    water

½ pint tomato
    purée
(1 teaspoon salt)

Cut up the hearts and put them in a casserole dish, cover with stock and tomato purée and cook gently at 375° for 1½ to 2 hours, or until tender. Blend the baby's portion with some of the juice.

STUFFED HEART

1 ox heart
6 oz wholemeal
    breadcrumbs
1 tablespoon
    chopped parsley
1 egg yolk

grated rind and
    juice of ½ lemon
1 grated onion
1 pint stock
(½ teaspoon salt)

Drain the trimmed and washed heart. Combine the ingredients for the stuffing and fill the heart cavities, pushing well down. Put in a casserole dish with the stock and cook gently at 375° for 2 to 3 hours, or until tender. Blend the baby's portion. Add a little of the stuffing and stock for older babies. This dish can also be roasted; either cook under foil for the first 2½ hours, turning and basting frequently, then without foil for half an hour; or parboil gently for about an hour then roast for 2 hours.

Tripe

Tripe is easy to digest and is ideal for children. It can be substituted, cut up and blanched (see below), for half the meat in many pie and casserole recipes.

TRIPE AU GRATIN

1 lb tripe
1 onion
2 tablespoons
  grated cheese
2 tablespoons
  wholemeal
  crumbs

juice of half a
  lemon
1 oz wholemeal
  flour
¼ pint milk
1 oz butter
(½ teaspoon salt)

Cut the tripe into strips. To blanch, put it into a saucepan, cover with cold water, bring to the boil and boil for 2 minutes; pour the water away. Cover the tripe with fresh water and the lemon juice. Add the chopped onion and simmer gently for 1 hour.

Make a sauce, either by heating the flour in the melted butter and then gradually stirring in the milk and ¼ pint of the tripe stock, or by making a paste with the flour and a little of the milk and then slowly stirring in the rest of the milk and the stock; then bring the whole to the boil. Put the tripe and onion into a fireproof dish, pour over the sauce, cover with the crumbs and grated cheese, dot with a little butter and brown under the grill. A serving of this makes a nourishing meal for an older baby already used to cheese and butter. For the younger baby, serve only the tripe, finely chopped or blended.

Tongue

Tongue is relatively cheap. It can be eaten hot or cold, and can be minced or blended to make a pâté. Add any seasonings after reserving the baby's portion.

BOILED OX TONGUE

Ox tongue is obtainable from most good butchers, and some butchers also stock small lamb's tongues.

Cover with cold water, bring to the boil and boil for 2 minutes. Pour away the water and cover with fresh. Simmer for about 3 to 4 hours, or until very tender, then remove skin. Blend or chop the baby's portion, according to age. Lamb's tongues would take about half the time.

Sweetbreads and brains

Sweetbreads and brains are nutritious and economical but you may have to search for a butcher who stocks them. They are difficult to come by but worth the trouble. Ask for calves' sweetbreads. They must be used within a day or two of purchase as they do not keep well. Soak them for a quarter of an hour, then blanch by putting them in fresh cold water and bringing to the boil.

STEWED SWEETBREADS

Cover prepared sweetbreads with water, add 1 tablespoon of lemon juice and bring to the boil. Lower
heat and simmer for 15 to 30 minutes. Remove mem-
branes, dice the baby's portion and blend. For the
older baby, a cream sauce can be added (see the
following recipe).

SWEETBREADS WITH CREAM SAUCE

sweetbreads (stewed   ½ pint milk
  as above)   (1 teaspoon salt,
1 oz butter or oil   pinch of
1 oz wholemeal   pepper)
  flour

Heat the butter or oil in a saucepan. Remove from
the heat and sprinkle in the flour. Stir till smooth;
return to heat and slowly pour in the milk combined
with the stock, still stirring constantly, and simmer
till thickened. Remove the baby's portion of sweetbreads and sauce, and blend together. Add seasoning
and sweetbreads to the remainder of the sauce.

BRAINS

Brains can be prepared in the same way as sweetbreads. Simmer them very slowly.

Mince

It is best, if possible, to buy stewing steak and mince it yourself, or an accommodating butcher will mince it for you.

COTTAGE PIE

1 lb mince
1 lb carrots
½ lb onions
1 tablespoon oil

1½ lb potatoes,
   cooked and
   mashed
1 pint water or stock
pinch mixed herbs
(½ teaspoon salt)

Brown the mince in the oil. Dice the carrots and onions and add them with the stock and herbs. Stew gently on top of the stove or in a covered casserole dish in the oven at 325° for about 1 hour, until the liquid is well reduced. Meanwhile, boil or steam and mash the potatoes. When the mince and vegetables are done, cover with the mashed potatoes and brown under a hot grill. Blend or mash the baby's portion.

MOUSSAKA

1 lb mince
½ pint tomato
   purée
½ lb onions
1 lb aubergines
1 tablespoon oil

½ pint stock or
   water
½ pint cheese sauce
   (see p. 87)
¼ lb cheese
(½ teaspoon salt)

Peel and slice the aubergines and steam until tender. Brown the mince in oil, then add the chopped onion with the tomato purée and liquid. Cook until the mince is thoroughly tender and the liquid well reduced; arrange aubergine slices on top. Cover with the cheese sauce, grate the cheese and sprinkle on top, and put in the oven or under the grill until the top bubbles. Blend, mash or chop the ingredients suitable for the baby.

SPAGHETTI WITH MEAT SAUCE

1 lb spaghetti
1 ½ lb tomatoes
1 pint of water or
    stock
pinch sage and
    thyme

½ lb mince
1 medium-sized
    onion
1 tablespoon oil
(½ teaspoon salt)

Brown the mince in a little oil. Skin and chop the tomatoes, dice the onion finely and add to the mince. Cover all the ingredients with water or stock and cook until tender (about three-quarters of an hour).

Use spaghetti made from buckwheat or hard wheat semolina available from health food shops. Cook in plenty of fast-boiling (slightly salted) water. (To prevent boiling over, add a tiny knob of butter or margarine to the water.) Cook until tender (10 to 15 minutes).

Blend or sieve the baby's portion.

STEAMED MEAT LOAF WITH GRAVY

Suet crust pastry
  (see p. 38)
1 lb mince
1 onion

1 carrot
1 tablespoon stock
(½ teaspoon salt)

Roll out the pastry. Mince the carrot and onion and add to the meat; moisten with the stock. Spread this mixture on the pastry, moisten the edges and join together. Roll up in cooking foil and steam for 2 hours, or bake at 375° for 1 hour. Serve with brown gravy (see below). Blend or chop the baby's portion, omitting the pastry for a young baby.

Gravy
2 oz butter or
  dripping
1 large tomato
1 small carrot
1 onion

2 oz wholemeal
  flour
pinch herbs
1 pint stock
(½ teaspoon salt)

Melt the fat, and lightly brown the sliced vegetables. Add the flour, stirring well, and fry to a rich golden brown. Add the stock and simmer for 30 minutes. Skim and sieve.

PASTIES

Suet crust pastry
  (see p. 38)
1 onion
1 lb mince

1 carrot
stock to cover
(½ teaspoon salt)

Lightly fry the mince. Chop the carrot and onion, add to the mince and simmer in a covered pan until the mince is cooked and the stock well reduced. Leave to cool.

Cut out circles of pastry using a saucer. Put a heaped tablespoon of the mixture on each round. Pinch the edges together. Lightly brush with milk or a little oil. Cook at 400° for about quarter of an hour, then reduce heat for a further quarter of an hour. For young babies omit the pastry and blend a little of the filling. (The meat from beef tea (p. 33) can be used in this recipe, minced or chopped with a little grated onion or carrot.)

BEEF STEW
(4-6 servings)

The cheaper cuts of beef can be very delicious, but need long, slow cooking.

1½ lb stewing steak
2 onions
½ lb carrots
2 oz dripping

1½ oz wholemeal or
  unbleached flour
1 pint stock or
  water
pinch thyme
(1 teaspoon salt)

Cut the meat into cubes. Dry it and dredge it in the flour. Heat the fat. Fry the meat until brown on all sides. Put it in a casserole dish with the diced vegetables. Pour in the stock and cook for about 2 hours at about 375°; or simmer slowly in a pan on top of the stove for the same time. You can save on utensils by adding a few diced potatoes, 20 minutes before the end of the cooking time. You may need to add a little more liquid. Blend or sieve the baby's portion.

Note: It is important to dry the meat well before flouring, and to have the fat really hot, as this seals in the juices

---

SPRING LAMB CASSEROLE

6 lamb chops
1 lb potatoes
½ lb carrots
½ pint water

½ lb onions
1 lb green peas or
  beans
(½ teaspoon salt)

Slice the vegetables, arrange all the ingredients except for the peas or beans in layers in a casserole dish, add the water, cover tightly and cook for about 1½ hours at 350°. Add the peas or beans half an hour before the end of the cooking time. Sieve, blend or chop the baby's portion.

IRISH STEW

1 lb boned neck or
   breast of lamb
1 lb potatoes
½ lb onions

1 tablespoon
   chopped parsley
water or stock
(½ teaspoon salt)

Cut the meat into small cubes, removing any fat or gristle. Peel and slice the potatoes and onions. Chop the parsley well. Put all the ingredients in layers in a casserole dish and add water or stock until the dish is three-quarters full. Cover and cook in a moderate oven (325°-350°) for 2 hours, or until the meat is tender. Blend or chop the baby's portion.

POACHED CHICKEN BREAST
(serves 1 or 2)

Some stores and butchers sell chicken breasts separately, or you can cut off a piece of breast for the baby and casserole or fry the rest of the chicken for the family.

¼ pint milk or
  stock
1 or 2 chicken
  breasts

1 tablespoon
  chopped parsley

Simmer the ingredients gently on top of the stove for about 15 minutes or until the chicken shows no trace of pink when cut. Remove the chicken and reduce the liquid to about 1 tablespoon by boiling. Blend the meat and reduced liquid for the baby.

CHICKEN OR RABBIT CASSEROLE

1 jointed chicken or
  rabbit
Juice of ½ lemon
½ pint milk or
  yoghourt

1 tablespoon
  chopped parsley
(½ teaspoon salt)

Arrange all the ingredients in a casserole dish and cook in the oven at 350° for 1 hour, or until tender. Blend or sieve the baby's portion. For older children and adults you can add button mushrooms and onions.

COCK-A-LEEKIE

1 chicken
6 leeks
1 oz butter or oil
2 tablespoons barley
2½ quarts stock or
water

a few sprigs of
thyme and
parsley
(½ teaspoon salt)

Joint the chicken. Wash the leeks thoroughly and chop finely. Heat the fat in a large saucepan and fry the pieces of chicken gently on both sides until golden, add the leeks and fry for a further 3 minutes. Pour on the stock, add the barley, thyme and parsley, bring to the boil, skim if necessary, and simmer for 2 hours or until the bird is tender. Remove the pieces of chicken, take out any bones and chop the meat, return to the soup, remove the thyme and parsley. Purée or sieve for a younger baby.

You can substitute rabbit for the chicken.

GREEN STEW

This is a very colourful dish, especially when served with buttered carrots or halved, grilled tomatoes, and appeals to children.

1 lb lamb, chicken or rabbit
½ lb courgettes or marrow
1 green pepper
1 bunch spring onions
½ lb green tomatoes
handful each of watercress and spinach
1 tablespoon oil
(1 teaspoon salt)

Wash and prepare the vegetables. Skin the tomatoes and chop them roughly. Peel and slice the courgettes or marrow. Chop the onions and pepper. Cut the meat into small cubes and brown them lightly in the oil. Then add the onions and pepper and stew over a low heat until they begin to soften. Now add the courgettes and tomatoes. Put the lid on the pan and simmer gently until the meat is tender and the vegetables cooked (half an hour to an hour, depending on the quality of the meat). Mince or liquidize the watercress and spinach and add to the pan. Cook for a minute or two longer. You should not need to add any water if you keep the heat low. Small new potatoes (about 1 lb) can be added at the same time as the courgettes and in this case you will need to add water – about ½ pint. Blend or sieve the baby's portion.

4. Fish

Fish is nourishing and easy to prepare, so introduce it soon after beginning weaning. You can blend or mash it with other vegetables such as potato or spinach.

Coley is probably the cheapest fish available – it is despised because of its rather dark flesh, but it is more delicate than cod (which it resembles) in texture and taste. It can be gently poached in water to which a small amount of lemon juice has been added, and this improves the colour. It should be very fresh.

Buy fresh fish from a reliable fishmonger whenever possible. Look for fish with bright bulging eyes and firm flesh – reject limp, scaling fish. Frozen fish will have lost some natural enzymes and may have chemicals added, so use it only in moderation.

Suitable fish and methods of preparation

Poach, steam, grill or bake: cod, haddock, sole, coley, plaice. After one year add trout, salmon, herring, mackerel, halibut and other oilier fish.

Do not give babies kippers, bloaters, smoked cod, haddock or salmon, salt cod, tinned sardines or tuna, taramasalata or other smoked, tinned or salted fish.

Never give shellfish to children under five, because of the danger of contamination and possible development of an allergy.

To prepare fish for babies under nine months old

1. Be sure the fish is well cooked.
2. Remove any skin or bone.
3. Put enough water or stock in the blender to cover the blades.
4. Dice the fish and add to the liquid.
5. Blend until the mixture is the desired consistency; or fish may be sieved. Do not add salt until you have removed the baby's portion.

When the baby is over nine months you may begin adding salt and other seasonings.

Steaming: Thin fillets of fish such as plaice, sole or fresh haddock can be steamed with a little milk and butter between two plates over a pan of boiling water.

Baking: All fish can be cooked in the oven. Use an ovenproof dish, well greased, or cooking foil wrapped loosely but securely round the fish to make a neat parcel. Fillets and small cutlets will take about 20 minutes at 375°. Give larger fish 15 to 20 minutes to the lb.

Poaching: When poaching fish use enough water to cover and make sure it is just simmering. *Never boil.* Add the juice of half a lemon to help keep the fish whole.

FISH PIE

1 lb cod, coley or fresh haddock	2 tablespoons unbleached flour
Juice of half a lemon	½ pint milk
1 lb mashed potatoes	(½ teaspoon salt)

Put the fish in a pan with the lemon juice and water to cover. Gently poach until the skin and bones come away easily. Drain the fish and keep the cooking liquid. Flake the fish, carefully remove all the bones, and arrange in an ovenproof dish. For the sauce, make a paste with the flour and a little of the milk, then stir in the rest of the milk and 1 cup of the stock, and bring to the boil. Pour over the fish, cover with the mashed potatoes and brown under the grill. Blend the baby's portion if all the ingredients are already familiar, otherwise set aside some of the fish for blending or puréeing.

CREAMED FISH

Prepare fish and sauce as above, put in small casserole dishes or shells, sprinkle with wholemeal crumbs, dot with butter and brown under grill.

FISH FLORENTINE

1 lb coley, cod or plaice fillets, or fresh haddock	½ lb cheese
	½ pint milk
	(½ teaspoon salt)
1 lb spinach	
1 tablespoon wholemeal flour	

Wash the spinach thoroughly under running water and steam until tender, or cook in a pan with no water except what remains on the spinach after washing. Stir frequently. Poach the fish according to the instructions on p. 58. Put the spinach in the bottom of an ovenproof dish and arrange the fish on top. Prepare a cheese sauce according to the recipe on p. 87 and pour it over the fish. Heat through in the oven or brown under the grill. For a younger baby, blend the suitable ingredients.

FISH LOAF

1 lb poached, flaked
   fish
4 tablespoons
   wholemeal
   crumbs
1 beaten egg or egg
   yolk

¼ pint milk
1 tablespoon
   chopped onion
(½ teaspoon salt)

Beat egg and milk and mix with the fish, crumbs and onion. Bake in a small, greased loaf tin for about 30 minutes at 350°. If all the ingredients are already part of the baby's diet, mash the baby's portion with a little boiled milk or stock.

KEDGEREE

½ lb brown
  unpolished rice
1 lb white fish,
  poached and
  flaked

2 eggs
2 oz butter
(½ teaspoon salt)

Wash the rice and cook in plenty of fast-boiling water. Hardboil the eggs and chop them. Melt the butter in a saucepan and add the rice, fish and eggs. Stir over a moderate flame until heated through. If your baby is not ready for whole eggs or rice, remove some of the fish before mixing and blend with a little of the poaching liquid.

SOFT HERRING ROE

Carefully grill the roe for about 3 minutes on each side. Try not to break the membrane which keeps it in shape. Alternatively poach it gently in a little milk for about 8 minutes. After cooking, remove the membrane, or press through a sieve, and serve with mashed potato or other vegetables; or for older babies, serve on toast.

5. Vegetables

One or two days a week can easily be made wholly or semi-vegetarian. Vegetable soup, with milk, cream, yoghourt or egg yolk added, followed by wholemeal bread and cheese, tomatoes or a green salad and fruit, makes a very well-balanced meal. Wheat germ or yeast extract added to the soup gives extra nourishment. Plenty of cheese, milk, eggs, wholemeal bread etc., ensures sufficient protein in a vegetarian meal.

A thick vegetable gravy made with vegetable stock and thickened with wholemeal flour or potato starch makes a good meatless sauce. For a cheese sauce recipe see p. 87. Any good vegetarian cookery book will provide many more recipes and ideas. Be careful to give the baby only those combinations suitable to his age and diet.

Try to serve fresh vegetables rather than frozen or tinned. For variety, cook and serve in different ways. Sprouts and cabbage can be chopped and served raw as a salad for older children and adults; sprouts, peas, carrots, parsnips etc. can be puréed and served with a little cream and nutmeg; parsnips can be roasted or baked; carrots, parsnips and turnips can all be glazed; onions can be boiled, fried, braised, roasted or stuffed. Really fresh vegetables are worth serving in the French manner as a separate course with melted butter and lemon juice, or a sauce.

Wash all vegetables carefully in warm water (if not grown organically they have probably been sprayed) and scrub or peel them. Cook without salt for babies under nine months.

Vegetables steamed, baked, casseroled or cooked in a *small* amount of water will retain their vitamins and minerals. The water can be used in gravies, stews or soups, or just as a drink.

Purée suitable vegetables for younger babies. Make sure the vegetables are not overcooked.

Suitable vegetables

Potatoes, carrots, spring greens, spinach, green beans, fresh peas, celery, parsnips, leeks, marrows, tomatoes, cauliflower and aubergines are all good first vegetables. Vegetables which may cause flatulence should be saved until the latter part of the baby's first year; they are broccoli, cabbage, beans, lentils, swedes, turnip, kohlrabi, Jerusalem artichokes, celeriac and dried pulses. However, since the pulses are both cheap and nourishing I have included a few recipes with the proviso that they should be given only to children over a year old.

Do not give the less digestible waxy or new potatoes to babies, only the old, floury sort.

Onion and garlic used as flavourings will do no harm, but do not give too much of the actual vegetable.

Puréed vegetables

For the young baby, the main meal may be simply a few teaspoons of puréed vegetables. To purée any suitable vegetable, pour into the blender half a cup of vegetable liquid, boiled milk or water to cover the blades. Add cooked vegetables gradually while blending on high speed. Soft vegetables can also be sieved or milled.

VEGETABLE SOUP

1 lb potatoes	1 large leek
2 large carrots	(salt)

Thoroughly wash, peel and chop the vegetables, and just cover them with water in a heavy pan. Bring to the boil and simmer until cooked. Blend or sieve, re-heat and serve with a knob of butter (and freshly ground black pepper, for adults). The soup should be thick, but can be thinned down with a little water for the young baby.

POTATO SOUP

1½ lb potatoes   water
1 clove garlic   ½ pint milk
1 bay leaf   (½ teaspoon salt)

Peel and chop the potatoes, put into a heavy pan with the garlic or onion and bay leaf and barely cover with water. Bring to the boil and then simmer until cooked. Blend or sieve. Add the milk and re-heat. This soup should be very thick, but thin down the baby's portion with a little more milk. Add black pepper and salt for adults.

WATERCRESS SOUP

1 lb potatoes
1 bunch watercress
1 onion
2 egg yolks

1½ pints water or
chicken stock
(½ teaspoon salt)

Peel and chop the potatoes and onion, wash the cress and throw away the ends of the stalks and any discoloured leaves. Bring potatoes and onion to the boil in water or stock. Simmer until cooked, then add the cress. Simmer a few moments longer before blending or sieving. Beat the egg yolks and add a little of the cooled soup. Pour this into the rest of the soup and re-heat gently, but do not boil.

SPINACH SOUP

1 lb spinach
1 onion
2 egg yolks or 1 cup
    yoghourt

1½ pints chicken
stock or water
(½ teaspoon salt)

Wash the spinach thoroughly under running water. Put in a pan with the chopped onion, add water or stock, bring it to the boil and simmer until tender. Blend or sieve. Add egg yolks (as in the previous recipe) or yoghourt in the same way.

Lettuce, sorrel, dandelion leaves, spring greens or turnip tops may be used instead of spinach.

FRESH PEA SOUP

2 lb peas
1 small head of
   lettuce
1½ pints water or
   chicken stock

small onion
1 carton yoghourt
mint
(½ teaspoon salt)

Pod peas, chop onion, wash lettuce and mint. Put the peas, onion and lettuce in a pan and cover with the water or stock. Stew gently until cooked. Sieve or blend. Mix the yoghourt with a little of the soup, and add this to the rest of the soup, stirring continuously. Re-heat, but do not boil. If the peas are young and fresh the pods (well washed) may be included. Sieve to remove the strings.

PALESTINE SOUP

(Unsuitable for babies under 1 year)

1½ lb Jerusalem artichokes	½ oz wholemeal flour
1 oz butter	½ pint milk
1½ pints boiling water or stock	(½ teaspoon salt)

Peel and slice the artichokes under water, as they discolour when exposed to the air, and lightly sauté them in the melted butter. Add the boiling water or stock, simmer for 30 minutes or until the artichokes are soft, and then sieve or blend. Mix the flour to a paste with a little of the milk and add to the soup. Bring it to the boil, stirring continuously, and simmer for about 10 minutes.

POMMES ANNA

2 lb potatoes	2 eggs or egg yolks
1 pint milk	clove of garlic
½ lb cheese	(½ teaspoon salt)

Peel and slice the potatoes very thinly and put them in cold water to avoid discolouration. Grate the cheese. Pound or crush the garlic. Beat the eggs or egg yolks and add the milk and garlic. Put the potatoes and cheese in layers in a casserole dish and pour over the eggs and milk. Dot with butter, and cook in a moderate oven (about 350°) for 1½ to 2 hours or until the potatoes are soft. Blend or mash the baby's portion.

VEGETABLE CASSEROLE

Use about ½ lb of some of the following vegetables:

potatoes	parsnips
onions	celeriac
carrots	Jerusalem
swedes	artichokes
celery	turnips

Other ingredients:

½ lb cheese	(½ teaspoon salt)
2 oz butter	

Wash, peel and slice the vegetables and arrange them in layers in a casserole dish. Pour in a cupful of water. Grate the cheese and sprinkle over. Dot with butter. Closely cover the dish with foil and put on a lid. Cook in a slow oven (about 325°) for 2 hours or until tender. Blend or mash the baby's portion, omitting any vegetables not suitable.

CAULIFLOWER CHEESE

1 cauliflower	1 tablespoon
½ lb cheese	wholemeal flour
½ pint milk	(½ teaspoon salt)

Discard the outer leaves and any discoloured ones, and wash well. Cut a deep cross in the stalk and put the cauliflower stalk downwards into a pan containing about an inch of water. Cover closely and cook until tender; the tougher stalk will be boiled and the tender florets steamed. Transfer to a casserole dish.

Make a cheese sauce with most of the cheese, according to the recipe on p. 87, using some of the cooking liquid in place of half the milk. Pour the sauce over the cauliflower, and sprinkle the rest of the grated cheese on top. Brown under the grill or in the oven. Blend, sieve or mash the baby's portion.

TOMATOES

If you have a home freezer, you can buy tomatoes when they are plentiful and cheap, and prepare a supply of tomato juice, soup and sauce for later use.

Wash the tomatoes well, quarter them and put them in a heavy pan over moderate heat, mashing them down slightly. Cover and cook, stirring occasionally until tender.

TOMATO JUICE

Pour the cooked tomatoes into a sieve and let the juice run through, without pushing, or attempting to purée it. The juice will be thin and a baby can easily drink it. For an older baby you can add a tiny pinch of salt. Freeze in ice cube trays, put in plastic bags and keep in the deep freeze.

TOMATO PURÉE

Sieve, or mill the pulp that is left over after preparing the juice. Freeze in the same way as the juice. These small amounts are useful for flavouring babies' individual dinners (see p. 81).

CREAM OF TOMATO SOUP

Heat together equal amounts of purée and milk. Do not boil. Season slightly for older babies.

RATATOUILLE

This vegetable stew in which the ingredients are simmered in oil is too rich for children under a year old, but when preparing it for the rest of the family you can put aside a small piece of each vegetable and simmer them gently in about 1 tablespoon of water until soft. Then sieve or mill.

72

½ lb onions

½ lb courgettes or
   marrow

½ lb aubergines

1 lb tomatoes

2 tablespoons oil

(½ teaspoon salt)

Wash, peel and slice the vegetables. Heat the oil in a heavy pan and melt the onions in it over a low heat. Add the other vegetables, cover the pan and simmer slowly until cooked (about half an hour).

DRIED PEA SOUP

(Unsuitable for babies under one year)

1 lb dried peas

1 onion, chopped

sprig of mint

1½ pints beef,
   mutton or ham
   stock

1 dessertspoon
   brown sugar

(½ teaspoon salt)

Wash the peas well, cover with boiling water and leave overnight. Next day, drain and rinse the peas, put them with the other ingredients into a casserole dish or heavy pan and cook slowly in the oven at 325°, or on top of the stove, for 2 hours or until soft.

Mill or sieve. The soup should be thick but can be thinned down with extra water or a little milk.

LENTIL SOUP

(Unsuitable for babies under one year.)

Substitute lentils for the peas and follow the above recipe omitting the mint and sugar. Choose green or brown lentils, not the orange sort.

CASSOULET

(Unsuitable for babies under one year.)

1 lb dried haricot beans	1 small onion
3 or 4 rabbit or chicken joints or	½ pint tomato purée
3 or 4 small lamb chops	(½ teaspoon salt)

Wash the beans well, cover with boiling water and soak overnight. Put into a large casserole and cover with fresh water. Add the chopped onion and the rest of the ingredients. Do not add salt until the end, as it hardens the beans. Put on lid and cook in the oven at 325° for 3 hours, or until tender. Check regularly as extra water may need to be added.

6. Eggs

Buy eggs as fresh as possible. Many health food shops stock free-range eggs and these are preferable to battery eggs. Some butchers also have fresh farm eggs. Never keep eggs too long, and if you put them in the refrigerator use the bottom shelf, not the space sometimes provided at the top of the door, as this is too cold.

A fresh egg broken into a saucer is compact and cushiony; the egg yolk remains intact and the white clings closely round it. A stale egg is runny, and the yolk is likely to break and mingle with the white.

For babies under eight months use only the yolk, and only hardboiled yolks, as these are easier to digest. There are many ways of separating eggs, but perhaps the most efficient is to break the egg and pour it from hand to hand letting the white run through your fingers into a bowl. The yolk is left in your hand free of white, and any membranous threads can be gently pulled off.

To softboil eggs for older babies put them into cold water, bring to the boil, turn off the heat and leave for one minute.

To hardboil eggs put them into cold water and boil for ten minutes. Plunge them into cold water when cooked. Hardboiled eggs can be mashed with other foods such as vegetables or fish.

BABY CUSTARD

1 egg yolk
1 tablespoon milk

Beat the yolk into the milk and steam, in a cup, in a small pan of simmering water, until set.

SCRAMBLED EGGS

(Use only the yolks for babies under eight months.) For each egg use a teaspoon of butter. Beat the eggs lightly, warm the butter in a small pan. Add the eggs, stirring gently. Remove the mixture from the heat before it is quite set and serve immediately. Be careful not to overcook. You can add a little chopped parsley or other fresh herbs for older babies.

POACHED EGG

Break the egg into a saucer. Simmer an inch of water in a small saucepan (a teaspoon of vinegar or lemon juice added will help to keep the egg together). Slip the egg gently into the pan and spoon the water over it or cover the pan. Cook until the white is set and serve on bits of buttered wholemeal toast, mashed potato or sieved spinach.

OMELETTE

1 egg
1 oz butter

Beat the egg lightly. Melt the butter in a small frying pan and add the egg. Remove from the heat before completely set and serve, cut into strips, with any creamed, mashed or blended vegetables.

FOAMY OMELETTE

2 eggs   1 tablespoon butter
2 tablespoons water

Separate the eggs and beat the yolks with the water until light and foamy. Beat the whites until stiff and fold into the yolks. Melt the butter in a frying pan, pour in the egg mixture, and cook over a low heat until the bottom is cooked, then put the pan under the grill on a low heat until the top is set and dry. (Or, if the oven is in use, put the pan on the bottom shelf for about 5 minutes.)

Served with a cheese sauce, cooked sieved tomatoes or blended vegetables, this makes a nourishing complete meal for an older baby.

FRENCH TOAST

1 egg   1 thick, crustless
1 oz butter   slice of whole-
                                meal bread

Soak the bread on both sides in the beaten egg, then fry it gently in the butter until just cooked, turning once. Serve cut into fingers. You can pour a little melted honey over them.

Cheese sandwiches can also be cooked in this way.

SPINACH CUSTARD

1 lb spinach   ½ pint milk
4 eggs   (½ teaspoon salt)

Wash the spinach well, cook in a little water, drain and chop very finely. Beat the eggs and milk and stir in the spinach. Cook in a casserole, or individual casseroles, in a moderate oven until the mixture is thoroughly hot and just beginning to set. For adults, serve with black pepper.

For older children and adults you can substitute three or four skinned and seeded tomatoes and a little lightly fried onion for the spinach.

7. *Individual Dinners*

The recipes suggested here for the baby alone are intended merely as a guide and the ingredients are more or less interchangeable.

While the preparation is simple, the small amount of liquid used in the cooking means that these meals cannot be left to take care of themselves. They cook very quickly, however, and none of the liquid is wasted. They can be followed by fruit or yoghourt, or any of the puddings given in chapter 10.

1 small potato	1 egg yolk and/or
1 small carrot	1 tablespoon
	grated cheese

Peel, wash and cut up the potato and carrot into small pieces, barely cover with water and cook for about 10 minutes, or until soft. Mash or blend with the cooking liquid. Return to the heat, add the yolk (and cheese), stirring briefly until the yolk is cooked but not hardened (and the cheese melted).

1 small potato (or	1 sprout
Jerusalem	1 soft herring roe
artichoke for	
the older baby)	

Peel and wash the potato or artichoke, wash the sprout well and finely chop both. Wash the roe and remove any loose membrane. Put all the ingredients together in a pan, cover with water and cook for about 10 minutes, or until soft. Blend or mash with the cooking liquid.

2 oz liver   1 tomato
1 potato

Peel and wash the potato, cut up all the ingredients, barely cover with water and cook for about 10 minutes, or until soft. Sieve or blend with the cooking liquid.

1 small fillet of   1 tablespoon milk
   plaice
2 sprouts

Wash the sprouts well and cut them up. Cook in a very small amount of water for about 10 minutes, or until soft. Add the milk to the sprouts and cooking liquid and simmer the plaice in it for about 5 minutes or until cooked. Mash or blend the ingredients together.

2 oz raw mince   1 tomato
½ stick of celery   1 potato
½ small onion   1 oz cooking oil or
                                                    butter

Wash and scrape the celery. Peel and wash the potato, onion and tomato. Lightly brown the mince in the cooking oil or butter, add the cut-up vegetables, barely cover with water and cook for about 15 minutes, or until soft. Sieve or blend with the cooking liquid.

1 medium-sized potato	2 teaspoons tomato purée
1 tablespoon cheese	1 teaspoon butter

Wash and scrub the potato well. Bake or steam it in its skin until soft. Remove the inside and mash with the other ingredients.

8. Cheese and Yoghourt

Cheese

Cheddar and other hard cheeses are formed by a process of coagulating milk with rennet, pressing the separated curd and ripening it. Pasteurized, processed cheese is a blend of aged and fresh cheeses melted and mixed with emulsifiers. It has a blander, less distinctive taste than natural cheese and generally contains preservatives and other additives. Pasteurization halts the ripening process, so that the cheese remains in the same state for a long time. Some of the natural hard cheeses now also have preservatives added, especially those pre-packaged by manufacturers or distributors,

Try to find a shop where you can buy unprocessed cheese cut from the wheel or block. The protein of natural cheese can be used pound for pound to replace that in meat.

Cottage cheese is an unripened, soft, natural cheese made from skimmed milk. Cream cheese is higher in calories and less suitable for small children.

Cheese spreads usually contain numerous additives such as gums, stabilizers and preservatives. They also have a high water content and less fat; some have flavourings added.

Yoghourt

Yoghourt is an ideal food for babies as it is easily digested. Buy only the plain kind and, if you wish, add your own fruit purées. A teaspoon of yoghourt and a teaspoon of mashed banana or apple purée provides an excellent first pudding. Yoghourt is also good added to some soups, casseroles and stews.

It is much cheaper to make your own yoghourt, and very simple once you acquire the knack.

BASIC RECIPE FOR MAKING YOGHOURT AT HOME

1. Bring one pint of milk nearly to boiling point and then cool to blood heat.
2. Gently whisk, beat or stir in one tablespoon of plain yoghourt.
3. Transfer to the container of your choice (a wide-necked vacuum flask if you have one) and cover.

4. Leave to set in a warm place overnight.
5. Cool and place in a refrigerator.

Note: Take care to make yoghourt under the most sterile conditions possible.

While yoghourt can be given in small quantities to babies as early as six months, it is advisable to leave cheese until your baby is at least eight months old.

HOME-MADE CHEESE SPREAD

¼ pint milk
1 egg
¾ lb cheddar cheese

(¼ teaspoon dry mustard)
(½ teaspoon salt)

Heat the milk in a double boiler over hot water. Beat the egg, grate the cheese and add them slowly (with the seasoning) to the milk, stirring constantly. Cook, stirring, for 15 minutes and cool. The spread can be stored in a covered jar in the refrigerator where it will keep for more than a week. Add a little onion juice or crushed garlic for older children.

HOME-MADE CHEESE SPREAD 2

Use cottage cheese and add a little onion juice, garlic, tomato purée, chopped fresh herbs or chives.

CHEESE SAUCE

½ lb cheese   1 tablespoon
½ pint milk   wholemeal flour

If the cheese is dry, grate it, if it is fresh and moist, dice it. Make a paste with the flour and a little of the milk, then gradually stir in the rest of the milk over the heat. Add the cheese and bring to the boil stirring constantly. Simmer until thick, and continue cooking for 10 to 15 minutes to make sure the flour is cooked through.

MACARONI CHEESE

½ lb macaroni   1 tablespoon flour
½ lb cheese   (½ teaspoon salt)
½ pint milk

Use macaroni made from millet, buckwheat or hard-wheat semolina, available from health food shops. Cook it in plenty of fast-boiling (slightly salted) water until tender. (To prevent boiling over, add a tiny knob of butter or margarine.) Drain the macaroni, mix it with cheese sauce, (see p. 87) and pour it into an ovenproof dish. Grate a little cheese on top and put it in the oven until the cheese has melted. Mash, sieve or chop the baby's portion.

CHEESE SOUFFLÉ WITH BREAD

1 small wholemeal
   loaf
½ pint milk
2 eggs

½ lb cheese
2 oz butter

Cut the crust off the loaf and break the bread into small pieces. (Dry and harden the crusts in the oven to use as rusks or to make breadcrumbs.) Put the pieces of bread in a buttered casserole dish. Boil the milk, pour it over the bread and mash with a fork until the bread is evenly soaked. Grate the cheese and separate the eggs. Stir the cheese, butter and yolks into the bread and milk. Beat the whites stiffly and fold them into the mixture. Bake at 325° for about

50 minutes until well risen and firm in the middle.

If your baby is already eating whole eggs and cheese, but is not yet ready for the rather dry texture of this dish, you can mash a little with some boiled milk.

CARROT CHEESE SOUFFLÉ

2 teaspoons wholemeal flour	2 oz grated cheese
2 oz butter	2 oz sieved cooked carrots
¼ pint milk	2 eggs

Melt the butter and blend in the flour. Pour in the milk gradually and stir until thick and smooth. Add the grated cheese and sieved carrots. Separate the eggs, beat the yolks and whisk the whites. Remove the mixture from the heat and stir in the yolks slowly before folding in the whites.

Pour the mixture into a buttered casserole dish and bake at 325° for about 50 minutes or until the middle is firm and a knife comes out clean. Mash the baby's portion with a little boiled milk.

Serve with a green vegetable.

9. Cereals

The introduction of cereals should be postponed until the baby is at least six months old in favour of high iron and protein foods, unless the doctor feels that a more filling food is necessary (see p. 26).

Look for natural grains whenever possible. Most health food shops have a wide range of untreated cereals. These may seem expensive, but since the grains are usually dried and flaked, you should find that in terms of weight they are good value for money.

To save time in preparation, look for untreated, whole-grain barley, oats, wheat, millet etc., which have been flaked or rolled for quick cooking. Since the whole grain is used, the nutritional value is not diminished.

Any cereal can be enriched by adding a tablespoon or so of nutritional yeast or wheat germ, or by cooking with milk, or milk and water, rather than water alone. To sweeten, use honey or puréed dried fruit.

The following recipes are measured in cups for the sake of convenience.

TOASTED WHEAT GERM

Put the raw wheat germ on a baking sheet and bake at 325° for 10 to 15 minutes, stirring occasionally. Store in an airtight jar; serve with milk and honey.

OATMEAL PORRIDGE

1 cup water or milk   ⅓ cup rolled oats
   (or half and half)

Put all the ingredients into a saucepan and cook over a moderate heat, stirring occasionally, until the mixture comes to the boil. Lower heat and simmer for 5 minutes. Remove from the stove, cover and allow to stand for a few minutes.

CREAM OF OATS

Follow the recipe above, but grind raw oats fine in a blender before adding to the liquid. Prepared in this way, the mixture is suitable for younger babies.

WHOLE WHEAT CEREAL

¼ cup flaked wheat   (¼ teaspoon salt)
1 cup water or milk

Sprinkle cereal into boiling water or milk, stirring constantly. Cook for 5 minutes or more to the desired consistency; stir occasionally. Remove from the heat and cover. Leave to set for a few minutes before serving.

MUESLI

Combine oats, wheat, millet, sultanas, nuts, wheat germ, dried milk, honey and any fresh fruit grated or chopped. Soak the cereal overnight and strain off excess water. Serve with milk. In this form, Muesli is only suitable for children of two and over. For babies, put half a dessertspoon with two dessert-spoons of milk in a pan, cook gently for five minutes, and sieve or blend.

10. Puddings

Though fresh fruit makes a perfect (and perfectly nutritious) ending to a meal, many traditional pudding recipes can be adapted so that they become a nourishing alternative to cheese or fresh fruit instead of being merely fattening.

Never oversweeten anything. Whenever possible use honey, or pulped and blended dried fruit as sweetener.

Most of the following recipes are intended for babies over eight months.

QUEEN OF PUDDINGS

1 small wholemeal
  loaf
2 eggs
½ pint milk

2 lemons
6 oz liquid honey
5 oz fruit purée

Cut the crusts off the loaf and break it into small pieces. Place them in a buttered casserole dish. Boil the milk and pour it over the bread, mashing with a fork to ensure it is soaked through. Separate the eggs and add the yolks to the bread and milk. Thinly grate the rind of the lemons and squeeze out the juice, add these to the mixture with most of the honey. Spread the purée over this mixture. Whip the egg whites until soft peaks form. Then add the rest of the liquid honey and continue whipping until stiff. Spread evenly over the purée. Bake in a low oven, about 325°, until lightly browned and crisp.

APPLE CHARLOTTE

1 lb cooking apples   4 oz honey
½ small wholemeal   ¼ pint water
  loaf
butter

Peel, core, and slice the apples, and gently stew them with the honey and water. Meanwhile, prepare thin, buttered, crustless slices of bread. Arrange most of them around the sides of a pudding basin, buttered side in, and put in the stewed apple. Arrange the rest of the bread on top, buttered side out. Trickle a little honey over and bake in a slow oven (about 325°) for 1 hour, until the top is well browned.

BAKED FRUIT WHIP

1 egg white
2 tablespoons honey
1 tablespoon lemon
   juice

4 tablespoons fruit
purée such as
apple or apricot
or pear

Beat the egg white until it is stiff but not dry, and gradually add the honey. Mix the fruit with the lemon juice and fold it into the egg white. Place in a greased baking dish in a pan of hot water. Bake at 300° for about 50 minutes or until the middle is firm.

QUICK CRUMBLE

1 lb sweetened,
   stewed, strained
   fruit
1 tablespoon wheat
   germ
1 tablespoon butter

2 tablespoons
ginger biscuit
crumbs (recipe
p. 107)

Put the fruit into a small greased baking dish. Mix wheat germ and crumbs and sprinkle them over the fruit. Dot with butter and bake at 350° for about 20 minutes or until nicely browned.

BAKED CUSTARD

1 pint milk	2 tablespoons
2 eggs	honey

Beat the eggs and add the milk and honey. Mix well and pour into a baking dish set in a pan of hot water. Bake at 325° on a low shelf of the oven for 1 hour or until set. Be careful not to overcook or the mixture will separate.

A LIGHT BREAD-AND-BUTTER PUDDING

1 pint milk	a few thin slices
2 eggs	crustless
2 tablespoons	wholemeal bread
honey	butter

Beat the eggs with the milk and add the honey. Put in a casserole dish. Butter the bread thinly and arrange it so that it floats on top of the custard. Bake at about 350° for approximately 40 minutes, until set.

RICE PUDDING

2 oz unpolished,
  round-grain rice
1 pint milk

¼ teaspoon
  cinnamon
3 tablespoons
  treacle

Mix the rice, milk, cinnamon and treacle in a buttered baking dish. Bake at 325° for 2 to 2½ hours, stirring occasionally.

11. Bread

Whenever possible buy wholemeal bread, either from a health food shop or from an old-fashioned baker. (Remember that some commercially produced 'brown' bread is made from coloured white flour.)

It is quite easy to make bread. You can make enough in one session to last a week as home-made bread does not go stale in the same way as bought bread. It also freezes well.

Apart from a large mixing bowl (a plastic washing-up bowl kept for the purpose serves very well), the main essential is an even warmth. The liquids used must be lukewarm (just at blood heat – if they are too hot they will kill the yeast), while the other ingredients should not be too cold or they will retard the rising action. So try to gather all the ingredients a couple of hours before starting, to let them warm up to room heat.

Knead most types of bread for about ten minutes on a floured board using a rolling and punching action with the heel of the hand. The dough should become smoother and less sticky. Cover it with a clean cloth and leave it to rise in a warm, draught-free place. Do not put it directly on a hot radiator or stove. If you have nowhere else, use an unheated oven with a large pan of hot water on the rack beneath. 80-85° is the ideal temperature for rising.

WHOLEMEAL BREAD

3 lb plain wholemeal
  flour
2 level tablespoons
  brown sugar
1 ½ pints warm
  water

1 oz dried baking
  yeast, or 2 oz
  fresh yeast
1 oz butter,
  vegetable fat or
  oil
1 level teaspoon
  salt

Stand the flour in a mixing bowl in a warm place. Dissolve I teaspoon of the sugar in ½ pint of warm water. Whisk the dried yeast into the sugar and water with a fork, or blend in the fresh yeast. Leave till frothy – about 10 minutes.

Rub the fat into the flour. If using oil, add when the dough is partially mixed. Dissolve the salt and remaining sugar in the rest of the warm water; add this and the yeast solution to the flour. Mix thoroughly to form a smooth dough. Working quickly to keep the dough warm, knead on a floured board until it is no longer sticky.

Cover the dough, and leave it in a warm place until it has doubled in size. Turn the risen dough on to a floured board and knead till firm. Divide the dough into 4 equal pieces, shape and put into well-greased 1 lb tins. Cover and leave aside in a warm place until the dough rises to about half an inch above the top of the tins. Bake the bread in a 450° oven or at gas mark 8, for 35 to 40 minutes. Remove from tins and allow to cool.

MALT BREAD

½ lb wholemeal flour

¼ pint warm water

2 oz black treacle

3 oz malt extract

3 oz sultanas or raisins

1 teaspoon baking powder

½ teaspoon bicarbonate of soda

1 egg

pinch salt

Mix the flour, water, treacle and malt extract. Leave in a warm place for 1 hour. Beat the egg and add to it the baking powder and bicarbonate of soda. Add this to the flour mixture, with the well-washed sultanas or raisins. Put into a well-greased 1 lb loaf tin and bake in a moderately hot oven 350° for 1 to 1½ hours. Remove from the tin and place on a rack to cool.

BABY BISCUITS

1 lb wholemeal flour
2 tablespoons soy
   flour
2 tablespoons non-
   fat dried milk
   powder

2 tablespoons
   wheat germ
2 tablespoons oil
3 tablespoons
   honey
(pinch salt)

Mix the dry ingredients together. Add the oil and honey and mix well. If necessary add a little water. Knead to a smooth ball and then roll out as thinly as possible on a floured surface. Cut into fingers and bake at 350° on a greased tin for 8 to 10 minutes until brown. Cool thoroughly and store in a tightly-lidded tin.

TEETHING BISCUITS

1 egg yolk
2 tablespoons honey
2 tablespoons black treacle
2 tablespoons oil
3 tablespoons wholemeal flour

1 tablespoon soy flour
1 tablespoon wheat germ
1 ½ tablespoons non-fat dried milk powder

Separate the egg and mix the yolk with the honey, treacle and oil. Add this to the dry ingredients. Roll the dough out very thinly on a floured surface and cut into small fingers. Bake at 350° for 15 minutes on an ungreased baking sheet. Cool thoroughly and store in a tightly-lidded tin.

12. *Cakes and Biscuits*

When visiting a child, most people unhesitatingly take a present of sweets or chocolate. Sweetstuffs are associated with holidays and festivities, are offered as bribes or rewards, and as a consolation when things go wrong. In this atmosphere, it would be almost impossible to raise a child without allowing him some sweetstuffs – the social and psychological drawbacks of attempting to do so would quickly outweigh the benefits. But you will begin with an immeasurable advantage if you prevent the development of a 'sweet tooth'. The following recipes will be found both satisfying and nourishing without relying solely on sweetness.

HONEYCAKE

6 oz butter or
margarine
½ lb honey
3 eggs – beaten

1 lb unbleached
flour
3 teaspoons baking
powder

½ teaspoon salt
¼ teaspoon
  bicarbonate of
  soda
¼ pint milk
1 teaspoon vanilla

2 teaspoons lemon
juice *or* grated
rind plus juice
of half an
orange

Cream butter or margarine and honey. Beat the eggs and add the milk. Mix and sift flour, baking powder, salt and soda. Add the dry ingredients to the butter and honey mixture alternately with the egg and milk. Add vanilla and lemon or orange juice. Pour into a prepared 8-inch cake tin. Bake at 375° for 30 minutes, then reduce the heat slightly for approximately 1 hour. The cake is cooked if the top springs back when touched. Cool for 10 minutes before turning out.

ORANGE FILLING

2 oz butter or
  margarine
3 oz honey
2 eggs, beaten
¼ pint orange juice

1 tablespoon grated
  orange rind
½ tablespoon
  lemon juice

Put all the ingredients together. Cook for 10 minutes over boiling water in a double boiler, stirring constantly. Fill the cake and put in the refrigerator.

Variations: use crushed, sieved strawberries, raspberries or other fruit juices in place of the orange juice.

GINGER CAKE

½ lb wholemeal flour
4 oz margarine
½ teaspoon baking powder
2 oz black treacle
2 oz golden syrup

4 oz Demerara sugar
1 egg
2 tablespoons milk
1 teaspoon ground ginger

Cream together the sugar and margarine. Slightly warm the treacle and syrup and add. Then add the beaten egg, flour and ground ginger. Dissolve the baking powder in the milk and stir well into the mixture. Grease an 8-inch square cake tin, or a 9-inch round one; line the bottom with grease-proof paper. Put in the mixture, smoothing over the top. Bake at 350° for 50 to 60 minutes.

CHEESE SCONES

½ lb wholemeal
  flour
2 oz grated cheese
1½ oz margarine

2 teaspoons baking
  powder
milk to mix

Rub the margarine into the flour and baking powder. Add the grated cheese and enough milk to make a stiff dough; it will need less than a quarter of a pint. Roll out and cut into rounds. Bake at 425° for 15 minutes.

NUT SCONES

½ lb wholemeal
  flour
2 oz ground nuts
1½ oz margarine

2 teaspoons baking
  powder
milk to mix
pinch salt

Rub the margarine into the flour. Add the baking powder and ground nuts and make into a stiff dough with milk. Roll out and cut into rounds and bake at 425° for 15 minutes.

GINGER BISCUITS

2 tablespoons
brown sugar
2 teaspoons baking
powder
1 teaspoon ground
ginger
1 teaspoon salt

1 lb wholemeal
flour
½ lb butter
3 tablespoons
black treacle

Sift the dry ingredients through a coarse sieve and mix them thoroughly. Rub in the butter until the mixture is the consistency of breadcrumbs. Add the treacle and knead well. Chill for an hour or two and then roll out thinly and cut into shapes. Bake at 375° for 8 to 10 minutes until lightly browned. Cool and store in a tightly-lidded tin.

OATMEAL BISCUITS

½ lb rolled oats
½ lb wholemeal
flour
1 teaspoon baking
powder

¼ teaspoon salt
2 oz butter
2 tablespoons
honey

Mix the dry ingredients together. Rub in the butter, add the honey and mix well. Grease a 9-inch baking tin and press the mixture into it. Bake at 350° for 10 to 15 minutes or until browned. Cool on rack. Cut into fingers.

NUT BISCUITS

½ lb wholemeal
  flour
3 tablespoons
  honey
4 oz butter
½ teaspoon salt

1 egg
6 oz finely chopped
  nuts
½ teaspoon baking
  powder

Sieve and mix the flour, salt and baking powder and rub in the butter. Beat the egg with the honey and add, mixing until smooth. Fold in the nuts. Put teaspoons of the mixture on a baking tin about an inch apart. Bake at 350° for about 10 minutes or until lightly browned. Cool on rack.

RUSKS

Cut whole-grain bread into half-inch thick slices and divide the slices into thirds. Bake at 250° for about 1 hour until dried-out and hard.

13. Drinks, Ices and Jellies

You can buy many natural, unsweetened fruit juices in health food shops, but these are usually expensive. If you have a liquidizer or juice extractor you can make your own. If not, the following recipes are a useful standby.

LEMONADE

2 lemons   1 ½ pints water
mild (e.g. clover)
  honey to taste

Wash the lemons and finely grate some of the rind. Squeeze out the juice and put it with the rind and honey into a jug. Add the water, stir well and leave it to steep for an hour or more. Stir again and strain.

ORANGEADE

Substitute 2 small oranges for one of the lemons in the previous recipe.

BERRY JUICES

Stew and strain any berries or combination of berries – such as raspberries, strawberries, redcurrants or blackcurrants, blackberries or gooseberries. Sweeten with honey and dilute with water to taste, or blend with milk. You can also simply blend and strain the raw fruit.

YOGHOURT ICE

½ pint yoghourt
honey to taste

½ lb fresh fruit,
mashed, blended
or grated

Half freeze the yoghourt. Remove from the freezer and beat well. Blend with the fruit and finish freezing. You can also serve the mixture without freezing as a pudding.

SIMPLE ICE CREAM

½ pint single	½ pint milk
cream or	5 tablespoons
evaporated milk	honey
2 eggs (or yolks)	1 pod vanilla

Beat the eggs or yolks lightly and stir in the honey. Simmer the milk with the vanilla pod, cool and add to the eggs, remove pod. Cook gently until the mixture will coat a spoon (be careful not to overheat). Whisk the cream or evaporated milk and fold it gently into the custard. Put it in the freezing tray and place in the freezing compartment of the refrigerator at its coldest setting. When half frozen, remove and beat well. Taste for sweetness and if necessary add more honey. Return to the refrigerator and freeze until set.

FRUIT JELLY

Soak 1 oz unflavoured gelatine in a quarter of a cup of water. Stand the cup in hot water to dissolve the gelatine. Cool slightly, and add it to 1¼ cups fruit juice, or 1½ cups fruit purée. Chill until set.

WATER ICE

1-2 teaspoons gelatine	½ pint fruit juice
1 tablespoon water	honey to taste
1 egg white	(a little lemon juice)

Dissolve the gelatine in the water and add it to the fruit juice and honey. Half freeze, stirring occasionally, then put it in a chilled mixing bowl, and fold in the very stiffly beaten egg white. Replace in the refrigerator and freeze.

14. Spreads

Try to avoid buying grocery jams – they are over-sweetened and artificially coloured, and generally contain additives. If you have to buy jam, look for the brands from Eastern Europe which usually contain only fruit and sugar. Home-made nut butters are also much better than the commercial variety. If the oil separates because they don't contain emulsifiers, just stir it back in before serving.

APPLE BUTTER

1 quart unsweetened
  apple juice
4 lb apples

2 tablespoons
  lemon juice
  (optional)
2 teaspoons ground
  cinnamon
  (optional)

If you use cooking apples you will need to use honey to sweeten. Boil the juice until it is well reduced.

Wash the apples well and cut them up. Add them to the juice and simmer, covered, over a low heat until they are tender. Put the mixture through a sieve or mill. Return to the heat and simmer uncovered, stirring frequently until the apple butter is sufficiently thickened. You can add up to 2 tablespoons of lemon juice or 2 teaspoons of ground cinnamon about 15 minutes before the mixture has finished cooking. If you need to sweeten it, add the honey now. Put into sterile jars and cover. The apple butter will keep in the refrigerator for up to a week, or you may freeze it in foil or plastic containers.

PEAR BUTTER

Make as above using pears and pear juice.

DRIED FRUIT BUTTER

2 lb dried fruit

Use any dried fruit or a mixture of fruit such as apricots, prunes, pears. Figs, dates, raisins or sultanas may be added in small amounts to sweeten. Wash the fruit and soak overnight in just enough boiling water to cover. Next day simmer (in the same water) covered, until tender (remove prune stones as they float up). Sieve or mill the fruit and add a little honey if necessary. Return to the heat and simmer until thick. Put into sterile jars (or foil containers) and cover. Freeze or use within a week.

NUT OR SEED BUTTER

(For children over one year old.)
Use any nuts or seeds – peanuts, pecans, walnuts, sesame seeds, sunflower seeds etc. Put 1 cup fresh roasted nuts or seeds in a blender, blend on high speed until well ground. Add a little peanut oil or other vegetable oil for a smoother consistency.

CARROT-PEANUT BUTTER SPREAD

Mix puréed carrots with an equal amount of peanut butter.

FRUIT-PEANUT BUTTER SPREAD

Mix finely chopped or puréed fruit with an equal amount of peanut butter.

Index

Index

Katharina Dalton

ONCE A MONTH

Once a month, with demoralising regularity, over fifty per cent of women feel tired, confused, irritable and incapacitated due to the effects of premenstrual tension. Many others are indirectly affected – husbands, children, colleagues, workmates and friends.

Premenstrual syndrome is responsible for the timing of half of all criminal offences in women, for half of all suicides, accidents in the home and on the roads, hospital admissions, incidents of baby battering and alcoholic bouts. These are the calculable effects – how much greater are the less obvious changes in a woman's daily life, in her behaviour, appearance and health?

The problems might seem insurmountable – but are they? This book is a popular and easily understood account of menstrual difficulties by a doctor with many years of professional and research experience in their causes and treatment. Katharina Dalton shows that in most cases women can treat themselves, and that in severer cases progesterone treatment can be highly effective. It is a book which many readers – male as well as female – will find informative, sympathetic, helpful and above all practical in relieving the suffering caused by premenstrual syndrome.

Harry Cole

POLICEMAN'S LOT

It's a policeman's lot to be involved with eccentric human behaviour and bizarre happenings, with personal dramas and social occasions, accidental disasters and deliberate wrong-doings. PC Cole, after nearly thirty years on the beat, has seen it all; and whether he's investigating the case of the exploding sewer cover or refereeing at a drunken Irish party, withstanding the abuse of the Gay Liberation Front or sorting out the imaginary fears of a lonely old man, it's his sense of humour that often seems the saving grace.

Helen Forrester

TWOPENCE TO CROSS
THE MERSEY

Helen Forrester tells the sad but never sentimental story of her childhood years, during which her family fell from genteel poverty to total destitution. In the depth of the Depression, mistakenly believing that work would be easier to find, they moved from the South of England to the slums of Liverpool. Here Helen Forrester, the eldest of seven children, experienced the worst degradations that being poor can bring. She writes about them without self-pity but rather with a rich sense of humour which makes her account of these grim days before the Welfare State funny as well as painful.

'The clarity with which utter privation is here recorded is of a rare kind' – Gillian Reynolds, *Guardian*

'. . . records, with remarkable steadiness and freedom from self-pity, the story of a childhood that – even if it was all forty years ago – most people would have set down in rage and despair' – Edward Blishen, *Books and Bookmen*

'. . . her restraint and humour in describing this stark history make it all the more moving' – *Daily Telegraph*

Fontana Paperbacks: Non-fiction

Fontana is a leading paperback publisher of non-fiction, both popular and academic. Below are some recent titles.

- ☐ CAPITALISM SINCE WORLD WAR II Philip Armstrong, Andrew Glyn and John Harrison £4.95
- ☐ ARISTOCRATS Robert Lacey £3.95
- ☐ PECULIAR PEOPLE Patrick Donovan £1.75
- ☐ A JOURNEY IN LADAKH Andrew Harvey £2.50
- ☐ ON THE PERIMETER Caroline Blackwood £1.95
- ☐ YOUNG CHILDREN LEARNING Barbara Tizard and Martin Hughes £2.95
- ☐ THE TRANQUILLIZER TRAP Joy Melville £1.95
- ☐ LIVING IN OVERDRIVE Clive Wood £2.50
- ☐ MIND AND MEDIA Patricia Marks Greenfield £2.50
- ☐ BETTER PROGRAMMING FOR YOUR COMMODORE 64 Henry Mullish and Dov Kruger £3.95
- ☐ NEW ADVENTURE SYSTEMS FOR THE SPECTRUM S. Robert Speel £3.95
- ☐ POLICEMAN'S PRELUDE Harry Cole £1.50
- ☐ SAS: THE JUNGLE FRONTIER Peter Dickens £2.50
- ☐ HOW TO WATCH CRICKET John Arlott £1.95
- ☐ SBS: THE INVISIBLE RAIDERS James Ladd £1.95
- ☐ THE NEW SOCIOLOGY OF MODERN BRITAIN Eric Butterworth and David Weir (eds.) £2.50
- ☐ BENNY John Burrowes £1.95
- ☐ ADORNO Martin Jay £2.50
- ☐ STRATEGY AND DIPLOMACY Paul Kennedy £3.95
- ☐ BEDSIDE SNOOKER Ray Reardon £2.95

You can buy Fontana paperbacks at your local bookshop or newsagent. Or you can order them from Fontana Paperbacks, Cash Sales Department, Box 29, Douglas, Isle of Man. Please send a cheque, postal or money order (not currency) worth the purchase price plus 15p per book for postage (maximum postage required is £3).

NAME (Block letters) _____

ADDRESS _____